EMMANUEL JOSEPH

The Humanitarian Ledger, Using Crypto to Fund and Secure Global Aid Efforts

Copyright © 2025 by Emmanuel Joseph

All rights reserved. No part of this publication may be reproduced, stored or transmitted in any form or by any means, electronic, mechanical, photocopying, recording, scanning, or otherwise without written permission from the publisher. It is illegal to copy this book, post it to a website, or distribute it by any other means without permission.

First edition

This book was professionally typeset on Reedsy. Find out more at reedsy.com

Contents

1 Chapter 1: The Dawn of a New Era   1
2 Chapter 2: The Mechanics of Crypto Aid   2
3 Chapter 3: Overcoming Skepticism   3
4 Chapter 4: Empowering Local Communities   4
5 Chapter 5: The Role of NGOs and Governments   5
6 Chapter 6: Case Studies in Crypto Aid   6
7 Chapter 7: The Ethical Considerations   7
8 Chapter 8: The Future of Crypto Aid   8
9 Chapter 9: Building a Global Movement   9
10 Chapter 10: The Challenges Ahead   10
11 Chapter 11: Lessons from the Field   11
12 Chapter 12: A Call to Action   12
13 Chapter 13: The Role of Education in Crypto Adoption   13
14 Chapter 14: Bridging the Digital Divide   14
15 Chapter 15: The Intersection of Crypto and Climate Action   15
16 Chapter 16: The Power of Decentralized Networks   16
17 Chapter 17: A Global Vision for Crypto Aid   17
18 Chapter 18: The Role of Transparency in Building Trust   18
19 Chapter 19: The Ethics of Crypto Philanthropy   19
20 Chapter 20: The Role of Women in Crypto Aid   20
21 Chapter 21: The Impact of Crypto on Local Economies   21
22 Chapter 22: The Role of Youth in Shaping the Future of...   22
23 Chapter 23: The Role of Art and Culture in Promoting Crypto...   23
24 Chapter 24: The Role of Academia in Advancing Crypto Aid   24
25 Chapter 25: The Role of Media in Shaping Public Perception   25

26 Chapter 26: The Role of Technology Companies in Driving...   26
27 Chapter 27: A Call for Global Collaboration   27

1

Chapter 1: The Dawn of a New Era

In a world increasingly driven by technology, the humanitarian sector has begun to embrace the transformative potential of cryptocurrency. Traditional aid systems, often plagued by inefficiencies, corruption, and delays, are being reimagined through the lens of blockchain technology. Cryptocurrencies, with their decentralized nature, offer a way to bypass bureaucratic hurdles and deliver aid directly to those in need. This chapter explores the origins of this shift, highlighting the early adopters who saw the potential of crypto to revolutionize global aid efforts. From disaster relief to long-term development projects, the possibilities are vast and inspiring.

The story begins with a small group of tech-savvy philanthropists who recognized the limitations of traditional banking systems in crisis zones. In regions where banks are inaccessible or untrustworthy, cryptocurrency provides a lifeline. By using digital wallets on smartphones, aid recipients can receive funds instantly, without the need for intermediaries. This innovation has already saved lives in war-torn countries and natural disaster areas, where time is of the essence. The chapter concludes with a call to action, urging more organizations to explore the potential of crypto in their missions.

2

Chapter 2: The Mechanics of Crypto Aid

Understanding how cryptocurrency works is essential for its effective implementation in humanitarian efforts. This chapter delves into the technical aspects of blockchain technology, explaining how it ensures transparency, security, and efficiency. Unlike traditional financial systems, where transactions can be delayed or manipulated, blockchain records every transaction in an immutable ledger. This transparency builds trust among donors, who can see exactly how their contributions are being used.

The chapter also explores the role of smart contracts in automating aid distribution. These self-executing contracts can be programmed to release funds only when certain conditions are met, such as the completion of a project milestone. This reduces the risk of mismanagement and ensures that aid reaches its intended recipients. Real-world examples, such as the use of crypto in Syrian refugee camps, illustrate the practical benefits of this technology. By the end of the chapter, readers will have a clear understanding of how crypto can streamline aid delivery.

3

Chapter 3: Overcoming Skepticism

Despite its potential, cryptocurrency faces significant skepticism, particularly from those who view it as volatile or speculative. This chapter addresses these concerns head-on, presenting evidence of crypto's stability and reliability in humanitarian contexts. It also highlights the efforts of organizations working to educate stakeholders about the benefits of crypto, dispelling myths and misconceptions.

One of the key challenges is regulatory uncertainty. Many governments are still grappling with how to regulate cryptocurrency, creating a patchwork of laws that can hinder its adoption. However, this chapter argues that collaboration between the crypto community and policymakers can lead to a more favorable environment for crypto aid. Case studies from countries that have successfully integrated crypto into their aid systems provide hope and inspiration. The chapter ends with a message of optimism, emphasizing that skepticism can be overcome through education and demonstration.

4

Chapter 4: Empowering Local Communities

Cryptocurrency has the power to empower local communities by giving them control over their financial resources. This chapter explores how crypto can be used to support grassroots initiatives, from small businesses to community-led development projects. By bypassing traditional financial institutions, crypto enables communities to access funding directly, fostering self-reliance and resilience.

The chapter also examines the role of crypto in promoting financial inclusion. In many parts of the world, people are excluded from the formal banking system due to lack of documentation or credit history. Cryptocurrency offers an alternative, allowing individuals to participate in the global economy. Stories of women in rural Africa using crypto to start businesses or farmers in South America receiving fair prices for their crops illustrate the transformative impact of this technology. The chapter concludes with a vision of a future where crypto empowers communities to shape their own destinies.

5

Chapter 5: The Role of NGOs and Governments

Non-governmental organizations (NGOs) and governments play a crucial role in the adoption of cryptocurrency for humanitarian purposes. This chapter explores how these entities can leverage crypto to enhance their aid efforts, from fundraising to distribution. NGOs, in particular, can benefit from the transparency and efficiency of blockchain technology, which can help them build trust with donors and stakeholders.

Governments, on the other hand, have the power to create an enabling environment for crypto aid. This includes developing clear regulations, investing in digital infrastructure, and promoting financial literacy. The chapter highlights successful partnerships between NGOs, governments, and the crypto community, showcasing how collaboration can lead to impactful outcomes. It also addresses the challenges of scaling up crypto aid, emphasizing the need for capacity building and innovation. The chapter ends with a call for greater cooperation among all stakeholders.

6

Chapter 6: Case Studies in Crypto Aid

This chapter presents a series of case studies that demonstrate the real-world impact of cryptocurrency in humanitarian efforts. From providing emergency relief after earthquakes to funding education programs in underserved communities, these stories illustrate the versatility of crypto. Each case study is accompanied by an analysis of the challenges faced and the lessons learned, providing valuable insights for future initiatives.

One notable example is the use of crypto to support Venezuelan refugees. With the country's economy in shambles, traditional aid channels were ineffective. Cryptocurrency provided a way to deliver funds directly to refugees, enabling them to purchase food, medicine, and other essentials. Another case study focuses on a blockchain-based platform that connects donors with local projects in real-time, ensuring transparency and accountability. These examples underscore the potential of crypto to transform humanitarian aid.

7

Chapter 7: The Ethical Considerations

As with any technology, the use of cryptocurrency in humanitarian efforts raises ethical questions. This chapter explores issues such as privacy, security, and the potential for misuse. While blockchain technology offers transparency, it also poses risks, such as the exposure of sensitive information. The chapter discusses strategies for mitigating these risks, including the use of privacy-focused cryptocurrencies and secure digital wallets.

Another ethical concern is the environmental impact of crypto mining, which consumes significant amounts of energy. The chapter examines the efforts of the crypto community to develop more sustainable practices, such as transitioning to proof-of-stake algorithms. It also considers the broader implications of crypto aid, such as its potential to disrupt traditional power structures. The chapter concludes with a call for a balanced approach that maximizes the benefits of crypto while minimizing its risks.

8

Chapter 8: The Future of Crypto Aid

L ooking ahead, the future of crypto aid is filled with promise. This chapter explores emerging trends and innovations that are shaping the field, from decentralized autonomous organizations (DAOs) to tokenized aid. These developments have the potential to further enhance the efficiency and impact of humanitarian efforts, creating new opportunities for collaboration and innovation.

The chapter also considers the role of artificial intelligence and machine learning in optimizing crypto aid. By analyzing data on aid distribution and recipient needs, these technologies can help organizations make more informed decisions. The chapter ends with a vision of a world where crypto is seamlessly integrated into the global aid system, enabling faster, more effective responses to crises.

9

Chapter 9: Building a Global Movement

The adoption of cryptocurrency in humanitarian efforts requires a global movement. This chapter explores how individuals, organizations, and governments can work together to promote the use of crypto for good. It highlights the importance of advocacy, education, and collaboration in building a supportive ecosystem for crypto aid.

The chapter also examines the role of social media and online communities in spreading awareness about crypto aid. By sharing success stories and best practices, these platforms can inspire others to join the movement. The chapter concludes with a call to action, urging readers to become ambassadors for crypto aid in their own communities.

10

Chapter 10: The Challenges Ahead

While the potential of crypto aid is immense, significant challenges remain. This chapter explores the obstacles that must be overcome, from regulatory hurdles to technological limitations. It also considers the broader societal implications of crypto aid, such as its impact on traditional financial systems and power dynamics.

One of the key challenges is ensuring that crypto aid is accessible to all, regardless of their technical expertise or resources. The chapter discusses strategies for bridging the digital divide, such as providing training and support to aid recipients. It also addresses the need for ongoing research and development to address the evolving challenges of crypto aid. The chapter ends with a message of resilience, emphasizing that the humanitarian sector has always been adept at overcoming adversity.

11

Chapter 11: Lessons from the Field

This chapter draws on the experiences of those who have implemented crypto aid projects, offering practical insights and advice. It covers topics such as project planning, stakeholder engagement, and risk management, providing a roadmap for others to follow. The chapter also includes reflections on the personal and professional growth that comes from working in this innovative field.

One of the key lessons is the importance of adaptability. In the fast-paced world of crypto, flexibility is essential for success. The chapter also emphasizes the value of collaboration, highlighting the role of partnerships in overcoming challenges and achieving impact. The chapter concludes with a reminder that the journey of crypto aid is just beginning, and there is much more to learn and discover.

12

Chapter 12: A Call to Action

The final chapter of the book is a rallying cry for readers to get involved in the crypto aid movement. It outlines practical steps that individuals and organizations can take to support the use of cryptocurrency in humanitarian efforts, from donating to crypto-based charities to advocating for policy changes. The chapter also encourages readers to think creatively about how they can contribute to the field, whether through technology, education, or advocacy.

The book ends with a vision of a future where crypto aid is a cornerstone of global humanitarian efforts, enabling faster, more effective responses to crises. It is a future where technology and compassion come together to create a better world for all. The final message is one of hope and determination, urging readers to join the movement and be part of the change.

13

Chapter 13: The Role of Education in Crypto Adoption

Education is a cornerstone of successful crypto adoption in humanitarian efforts. This chapter explores the importance of educating both aid workers and recipients about the benefits and functionalities of cryptocurrency. Many people are hesitant to embrace crypto due to a lack of understanding or fear of the unknown. By providing clear, accessible resources and training programs, organizations can demystify crypto and build confidence in its use.

The chapter highlights innovative educational initiatives, such as workshops in refugee camps and online courses for aid workers. These programs not only teach the basics of blockchain technology but also emphasize its practical applications in real-world scenarios. For example, a farmer in a remote village can learn how to use a digital wallet to receive payments for their crops, bypassing exploitative middlemen. The chapter concludes by stressing that education is not a one-time effort but an ongoing process that must evolve with the technology.

14

Chapter 14: Bridging the Digital Divide

While cryptocurrency holds immense promise, its effectiveness is limited by the digital divide—the gap between those who have access to technology and those who do not. This chapter examines the challenges of implementing crypto aid in regions with limited internet connectivity or technological infrastructure. It also explores potential solutions, such as the development of offline crypto transactions and the use of low-cost, solar-powered devices.

The chapter also discusses the importance of inclusivity in crypto aid initiatives. For example, women and marginalized communities often face additional barriers to accessing technology. By designing programs that specifically address these barriers, organizations can ensure that crypto aid reaches the most vulnerable populations. The chapter ends with a call for global collaboration to bridge the digital divide, emphasizing that no one should be left behind in the crypto revolution.

15

Chapter 15: The Intersection of Crypto and Climate Action

Cryptocurrency is increasingly being used to support climate action and environmental sustainability, two critical components of humanitarian efforts. This chapter explores how blockchain technology can track and verify carbon credits, fund reforestation projects, and support renewable energy initiatives. By providing transparency and accountability, crypto can help ensure that climate funds are used effectively and reach their intended destinations.

The chapter also examines the environmental concerns associated with crypto mining, particularly its energy consumption. It highlights efforts by the crypto community to transition to more sustainable practices, such as using renewable energy sources and developing energy-efficient algorithms. The chapter concludes with a vision of a future where crypto not only funds climate action but also operates in harmony with the planet.

16

Chapter 16: The Power of Decentralized Networks

Decentralization is one of the core principles of cryptocurrency, and it has profound implications for humanitarian aid. This chapter explores how decentralized networks can empower individuals and communities to take control of their own aid efforts. Unlike traditional systems, where decisions are made by a central authority, decentralized networks distribute power among all participants, fostering collaboration and innovation.

The chapter also examines the role of decentralized autonomous organizations (DAOs) in humanitarian aid. These organizations operate on blockchain technology and are governed by smart contracts, enabling transparent and democratic decision-making. For example, a DAO could be created to manage funds for a community-led development project, with all stakeholders having a say in how the funds are used. The chapter ends with a discussion of the challenges and opportunities of decentralization, emphasizing its potential to create more equitable and effective aid systems.

17

Chapter 17: A Global Vision for Crypto Aid

The final chapter of the book looks to the future, envisioning a world where cryptocurrency is fully integrated into global humanitarian efforts. It explores the potential for crypto to create a more connected, transparent, and efficient aid system, one that can respond to crises in real-time and empower communities to build a better future. The chapter also considers the role of emerging technologies, such as artificial intelligence and the Internet of Things, in enhancing the impact of crypto aid.

The chapter concludes with a call for unity and collaboration. The challenges facing humanity—from climate change to inequality—are too great for any one organization or technology to solve alone. By working together, the crypto community, humanitarian organizations, governments, and individuals can create a brighter future for all. The book ends with a message of hope, urging readers to embrace the potential of crypto and join the movement to transform global aid efforts.

18

Chapter 18: The Role of Transparency in Building Trust

Transparency is a cornerstone of effective humanitarian aid, and cryptocurrency offers unparalleled opportunities to enhance it. This chapter delves into how blockchain technology can provide a clear, immutable record of every transaction, ensuring that donors and stakeholders can track the flow of funds with precision. This level of transparency not only builds trust but also reduces the risk of corruption and mismanagement, which have long plagued traditional aid systems.

The chapter explores real-world examples where crypto has been used to create transparent aid systems. For instance, during a recent disaster, a blockchain-based platform allowed donors to see exactly how their contributions were being used, from the purchase of supplies to their delivery on the ground. This level of accountability has the potential to revolutionize donor confidence and increase funding for critical projects. The chapter concludes by emphasizing that transparency is not just a technical feature but a moral imperative in humanitarian work.

19

Chapter 19: The Ethics of Crypto Philanthropy

As cryptocurrency becomes more integrated into humanitarian efforts, ethical considerations must be addressed. This chapter examines the moral implications of using crypto for aid, including issues of equity, access, and power dynamics. While crypto can democratize aid distribution, it also raises questions about who controls the technology and who benefits from it.

The chapter also discusses the ethical responsibilities of crypto philanthropists and organizations. For example, how should they ensure that their efforts do not inadvertently exacerbate existing inequalities? What safeguards are needed to protect vulnerable populations from exploitation? The chapter concludes with a call for a code of ethics specific to crypto philanthropy, one that prioritizes fairness, inclusivity, and accountability.

20

Chapter 20: The Role of Women in Crypto Aid

Women play a crucial role in humanitarian efforts, yet they are often underrepresented in the tech and crypto sectors. This chapter explores how empowering women with crypto knowledge and resources can amplify the impact of aid initiatives. From female entrepreneurs using crypto to start businesses to mothers receiving direct aid for their families, the potential for positive change is immense.

The chapter highlights successful programs that have trained women in blockchain technology, enabling them to take on leadership roles in their communities. It also examines the unique challenges women face in accessing crypto, such as limited digital literacy and societal barriers. The chapter concludes with a vision of a future where women are at the forefront of the crypto aid movement, driving innovation and creating lasting change.

21

Chapter 21: The Impact of Crypto on Local Economies

C ryptocurrency has the potential to transform local economies, particularly in regions affected by conflict or economic instability. This chapter explores how crypto can provide a stable alternative to volatile local currencies, enabling businesses to thrive and communities to rebuild. By bypassing traditional financial systems, crypto can also reduce dependency on foreign aid and foster self-sufficiency.

The chapter includes case studies of communities that have successfully integrated crypto into their local economies. For example, a small town in a developing country used crypto to create a local marketplace, where goods and services could be traded without the need for cash. This not only boosted the local economy but also provided a sense of security and stability for residents. The chapter concludes by emphasizing the importance of supporting local initiatives that leverage crypto for economic development.

22

Chapter 22: The Role of Youth in Shaping the Future of Crypto Aid

Young people are the future of the crypto aid movement, bringing fresh perspectives and innovative ideas. This chapter explores how youth-led initiatives are using cryptocurrency to address global challenges, from climate change to education. By engaging young people in the development and implementation of crypto aid projects, organizations can ensure that their efforts are relevant and impactful.

The chapter highlights examples of youth-driven crypto projects, such as a student-led initiative that uses blockchain to fund scholarships for underprivileged students. It also discusses the importance of providing young people with the tools and resources they need to succeed in the crypto space, from education to mentorship. The chapter concludes with a call to action, urging organizations to invest in the next generation of crypto leaders.

Chapter 23: The Role of Art and Culture in Promoting Crypto Aid

Art and culture have the power to inspire and mobilize people, making them valuable tools in the promotion of crypto aid. This chapter explores how artists and cultural leaders are using their platforms to raise awareness about the potential of cryptocurrency in humanitarian efforts. From digital art auctions to blockchain-based storytelling, the possibilities are endless.

The chapter includes examples of successful art and culture initiatives that have supported crypto aid. For instance, a global art project used blockchain to verify the authenticity of artworks, with proceeds going to humanitarian causes. The chapter also discusses the role of cultural narratives in shaping public perception of crypto, emphasizing the need for positive and inclusive stories. The chapter concludes with a vision of a future where art and culture are integral to the crypto aid movement.

24

Chapter 24: The Role of Academia in Advancing Crypto Aid

Academic institutions play a crucial role in advancing the field of crypto aid through research, education, and innovation. This chapter explores how universities and research centers are contributing to the development of blockchain technology and its applications in humanitarian efforts. From conducting studies on the impact of crypto aid to developing new tools and platforms, academia is at the forefront of this emerging field.

The chapter highlights successful collaborations between academic institutions and humanitarian organizations. For example, a university research team developed a blockchain-based platform for tracking aid distribution, which has been adopted by several NGOs. The chapter also discusses the importance of interdisciplinary approaches, bringing together experts from fields such as computer science, economics, and social work. The chapter concludes with a call for increased investment in academic research on crypto aid.

25

Chapter 25: The Role of Media in Shaping Public Perception

Media plays a critical role in shaping public perception of cryptocurrency and its potential in humanitarian efforts. This chapter explores how media coverage can influence the adoption and success of crypto aid initiatives. Positive stories can inspire trust and support, while negative coverage can create skepticism and resistance.

The chapter examines the role of different types of media, from traditional news outlets to social media platforms, in promoting crypto aid. It also discusses the importance of accurate and balanced reporting, particularly in addressing misconceptions about crypto. The chapter includes examples of successful media campaigns that have raised awareness and funding for crypto aid projects. The chapter concludes with a call for responsible journalism that highlights the potential of crypto to create positive change.

26

Chapter 26: The Role of Technology Companies in Driving Innovation

Technology companies are key drivers of innovation in the crypto aid space, developing new tools and platforms that enhance the effectiveness of humanitarian efforts. This chapter explores how tech companies are collaborating with humanitarian organizations to create solutions that address real-world challenges. From blockchain-based identity systems to AI-powered aid distribution platforms, the possibilities are vast.

The chapter highlights successful partnerships between tech companies and NGOs, showcasing how these collaborations have led to impactful outcomes. For example, a tech company developed a blockchain-based system for verifying the identities of refugees, enabling them to access aid and services more easily. The chapter also discusses the importance of ethical considerations in tech development, ensuring that innovations are inclusive and equitable. The chapter concludes with a vision of a future where technology companies are integral to the crypto aid movement.

27

Chapter 27: A Call for Global Collaboration

The final chapter of the book emphasizes the importance of global collaboration in advancing the crypto aid movement. It explores how individuals, organizations, governments, and tech companies can work together to create a more connected, transparent, and effective aid system. By sharing knowledge, resources, and best practices, stakeholders can overcome challenges and maximize the impact of their efforts.

The chapter includes examples of successful global collaborations, such as a coalition of NGOs, tech companies, and governments that used crypto to respond to a major disaster. It also discusses the role of international organizations, such as the United Nations, in promoting the adoption of crypto aid. The chapter concludes with a message of hope and unity, urging readers to join the global movement to transform humanitarian efforts through cryptocurrency. The book ends with a vision of a future where crypto aid is a cornerstone of global humanitarian efforts, enabling faster, more effective responses to crises and creating a better world for all.

Book Description: "The Humanitarian Ledger: Using Crypto to Fund and Secure Global Aid Efforts"

In a world grappling with crises—war, poverty, climate change, and natural disasters—the need for efficient, transparent, and impactful humanitarian aid has never been greater. Yet, traditional systems of aid delivery are often hindered by bureaucracy, corruption, and inefficiency, leaving millions without the help they desperately need. Enter cryptocurrency and blockchain technology, a groundbreaking innovation that is reshaping the way we think about global aid.

The Humanitarian Ledger: Using Crypto to Fund and Secure Global Aid Efforts is a compelling exploration of how cryptocurrency is transforming the humanitarian sector. This book takes readers on a journey through the origins, mechanics, and real-world applications of crypto in aid efforts, offering a vision of a future where technology and compassion intersect to create lasting change.

From empowering local communities to ensuring transparency and accountability, this book delves into the myriad ways crypto is being used to address some of the world's most pressing challenges. It examines the role of NGOs, governments, tech companies, and grassroots movements in driving this transformation, while also addressing the ethical considerations and challenges that come with adopting such a disruptive technology.

Through vivid case studies, personal stories, and expert insights, *The Humanitarian Ledger* illustrates how crypto is already making a difference—whether it's delivering emergency funds to refugees, supporting climate action, or enabling financial inclusion for the unbanked. It also looks ahead to the future, exploring emerging trends like decentralized autonomous organizations (DAOs), tokenized aid, and the integration of artificial intelligence.

But this book is more than just a technical guide or a collection of success stories. It's a call to action. It challenges readers to rethink the status quo, embrace innovation, and join a global movement that is redefining what it means to give and receive aid. Whether you're a tech enthusiast, a humanitarian worker, a policymaker, or simply someone who cares about making the world a better place, *The Humanitarian Ledger* offers inspiration, insight, and practical guidance for harnessing the power of crypto to create a more equitable and compassionate world.

At its core, this book is a testament to the resilience of the human spirit and the transformative potential of technology. It's a story of hope, collaboration,

CHAPTER 27: A CALL FOR GLOBAL COLLABORATION

and the belief that, together, we can build a future where aid is not just a temporary fix but a pathway to lasting empowerment. *The Humanitarian Ledger* is your guide to understanding and participating in this revolutionary shift—one block at a time.